The Amazing Adventures of StampyLonghead

2

StampyLonghead and the Gnomes is an original work of fan fiction. It is not associated with, approved, or endorsed by Minecraft or MojangAB.

Minecraft is the official trademark of MojangAB

Don't forget to check our latest Best Sellers from

Innovate Media:

Table of Contents

Introduction

Stampylonghead the cat has a new motto in life namely, 'eat, sleep, adventure, eat, sleep, eat, sleep'. He believes to appreciate the joy of eating and sleeping, going on an adventure once in a while is a good thing to do. As a result he decides to go looking for an adventure. On his way he comes across the village of Tuk Tuk which means slow and steady. The village seems like a very nice place with nice folks. It has tall walls of strong blocks and an army to defend it when the need calls. Stampy decides to spend some time in the village, which happens to be located right next to river called Doubtfire. There is a dense forest surrounding the village from three sides. The forest is very important for the people for food and wood.

Here, he befriends Lola the bird, who works as the town's advisor on all matters, and Sprinter Joyride (a.k.a. Flash) the turtle. Flash is the General of the Tuk Tuk army, which comprises entirely of hares who are chosen for their speed. Stampy really likes Flash the turtle because even though he is slow, thinks he is as fast as a lightning. This was a problem for the Tuk Tuk army and angered the general and the soldiers. Stampy, however, is good friends with Flash, because Stampy likes taking things slow and easy.

Lola, on the other hand, is a nagging bird who seems to believe that she is the best at everything, although everything she gets involved in ends up in a disaster. Folks call her Plumpy because of her love for baking and eating cakes, but apart from that she is very caring and hospitable towards everybody, which sets in well with Stampy as it means a nonstop supply of delicious cakes.

Stampy became popular in a few months but he is having a hard time maintaining it. Everybody in the village looks up to him and considers him to be the final authority on every matter. The attention along with free cake, and plenty of time to rest seems to agree with Stampy. He even suggested changing the name of the village to Stampville, but no one liked it.

The folk of Tuk Tuk usually are a very hospitable bunch. But they consider everything from the river to the forest to be their property, and guard it jealously. They recently received word that a tribe of gnomes was seen, coming their way led by a gnome warrior princess named Gnelissa and equipped with weapons for combat. This news reached the village and made everyone worried.

Chapter 1:

The Uninvited Guests

'Did you hear about the gnomes, Stampy?' Flash asked an indifferent Stampy, in a deep worried voice.

"I sure did," Stampy replied while dreamily gazing at the door, waiting for Lola to bring his cake.

"What do you reckon we do about it?" asked Flash, barely concealing his excitement at the prospect of a potential battle. "If it was up to me I would rush down there right now, destroy that foolish bunch of gnomes, and still make it back in time for dinner." Stampy looked at him with raised eyebrows.

Flash would never admit to being slow: his determination had got him to the rank of general in the Tuk Tuk army. It's actually a fun story. Flash had regularly applied for the army for a total of four years, but he had been rejected for obvious reasons. The previous General always teased Flash about being slow but Flash never accepted that, because for him he was as fast as anyone else, or perhaps a tad bit quicker. At his fourth recruitment attempt, the General went a bit too far and decided to embarrass Flash in front of the entire village. General Rover, as he was called, took Flash to the village market and made a laughingstock out of him, stating that the only way Flash could get in the army is if he gets out of his shell and hops around like a rabbit. This was the height of humiliation for Mr. Sprinter (Flash) as the shell is the sign of respect in the turtle community and mimicking a rabbit is considered to be the highest offence.

Angered by the General's statement Flash challenged him to a speed contest on the terms that if Flash wins he will not only get into the army but will be made General. But if the General wins Flash will have to face the humiliation of removing his shell and mimicking a rabbit's hop.

The challenge was simple - whoever reaches his home the quickest wins.

Laughing hysterically, General Rover accepted the challenge, while boasting, "Sprinter, you fool, my house is just around the corner from the market whereas you rest under the tree located at the far end of the village. It won't be fair to you, so it's only fair that you make for my house and I race towards your tree, and to make it even simpler I will race to and from your tree ten times, but you just have to reach my place once before my tenth round. How does that sound?" concluded the General in fits of laughter.

"I believe that will not be fair to you General. Therefore, I suggest we stick to our old bargain," replied Flash in a calm tone and the General, laughing louder, agreed to this.

The race was scheduled for the very next day and everybody was certain that General Rover, being the fastest hare in the village would beat Flash and that Flash was a fool to suggest such a thing. The time finally came for the race with everyone cheering for the General, while Lola the bird was the only one supporting Flash. Everyone seemed certain about Flash's humiliation, everyone except Flash; he wore an expression as if he had already won the race.

The whistle sounded loud and clear and General Rover ran towards his house as swiftly as possible, all eyes following him, nobody cared about Flash and within minutes the general had reached his place and supposedly won. It was at this point that everyone turned to look at Flash and was surprised. He was hiding in his shell.

"Come out sprinter, you have lost and it's time to pay the price!!" exclaimed the general.

"Lost? I don't think you understand, Rover," Flash replied.

"The challenge was that whoever reached his home fastest would win. You assumed that my home is by the tree where you had found me resting a few days back while in fact my home is my shell and I believe I was the first one to reach my house as I was in my shell soon after the whistle sounded," Flash concluded with a smile.

The General was completely lost for words and he could not believe that he had been fooled by a turtle. Nonetheless, he had given his word and the village folk expected him to honor it, as a result Flash became the General and gained everyone's respect while earning the name of 'Flash' for his quick wits.

Stampy had heard this story a million times from Flash, and every time the new version was more exaggerated than the last.

"I knew that oaf could never beat me, I would have humiliated the poor guy even more if I raced him head to head. As a result I thought to outsmart him instead of beating at his own game," Flash claimed. Stampy could not help but smile.

"It was nice of you to spare him the shame," Stampy replied sarcastically, but Flash took it as a complement, missing the point altogether.

At that very moment there was a knock on the door. "Come in Lola," pronounced Stampy, and there was Lola with Stampy's cake.

"I have been worried sick with all the gnome talk going on the village. Everybody thinks they are coming for our land," stated Lola as soon as she entered the room.

"I don't know what you people are waiting for. I suggest that we send them my freshly baked cakes which ought to soften them up. Besides, I hear they are being led by their princess Gnelissa. I am sure she would appreciate this gesture and leave us alone."

All this discussion was annoying Stampy as, being a cat, he was not very fond of gnomes.

"Why don't you say anything Stampy? Does it not bother you that they are coming this way?" asked Lola.

The fact of the matter was that initially Stampy did not care about the gnomes. However, when he realized that the gnomes might disturb his great life he started taking it seriously.

"I believe neither cakes would do us any good nor a fight, I have something else in mind. Flash, why don't you gather the villagers in the village market by noon, I wish to present a solution to this problem."

Immediately, sensing the tone, Flash headed towards the door as swiftly as possible.

"I don't think you considered my idea carefully, Stampy," Lola went on.

"You never heed what I have to say. I am telling you cakes are the answer to this problem. Your solution will not matter to them if you don't present them with my cakes, they won't even listen to you, and then you will be sorry for not paying attention to me," Lola concluded.

Stampy hurriedly finished his cake as he did not want to listen to Lola all day, but just as he got up and turned towards the door, "Flash, what are you still doing here? It's almost noon and you were supposed to inform everybody to meet me at the village market," said an irritable Stampy.

"I am going, don't worry about it, I will inform everybody in no time," explained an upbeat Flash, although he had barely covered half the distance to the door.

"Lola, could you please take care of this?" Stampy said turning to Lola.

"Flash, why don't you go to your soldiers and prepare a small group for the meeting with the gnomes tonight," Stampy asked.

At noon, thanks to Lola, everybody was gathered in the market place. "I believe, that a battle is not in our interest, therefore, I suggest that we hear out the gnomes and if they have come looking for a place to stay, we can offer them our forest on the condition that they cannot enter the village but we can enter the forest at will," explained Stampy.

Stampy already knew that they would agree to his suggestion but still he wanted their consent before proceeding. The villagers agreed with Stampy and in the evening Stampy headed towards the outskirts along with the soldiers.

Chapter 2:

The Truce

Stampy was quite sure that his suggestion would work. He had learned to trust his decisions during his stay at Tuk Tuk. He was always trusted by the villagers and they always accepted his decisions.

While riding out to meet the gnome party Stampy was a bit nervous, because he had to conceal his disliking for the gnomes, otherwise this deal would never take place. The meeting place which Stampy had decided was far away from the village and at a considerable distance from the forest. He had never met gnomes before but whatever he had heard about them was enough to dislike them.

He knew they disliked cats, he knew they can fight well when challenged and he knew that they are fond of mischief but, nonetheless, he had to tolerate them today because it was in the interest of the village. Along with his small group of soldiers, Stampy stood waiting for the gnomes with one hand on his sword. He knew from the reports that it was a large party of gnomes travelling at a great pace. Therefore he did not feel the need to make camp as he thought the deal with the gnomes would be done before nightfall.

It had only been a little while before the gnome party came into sight. Stampy realized that he had not expected such a large number of gnomes but still it did not matter, he thought to himself, as he was there with a peace proposition. As the gnomes saw Stampy and his small group, they slowed down in caution and every gnome reached for the hilt of his sword, as if expecting an attack. They came to a halt at a considerable distance from Stampy and his soldiers, as if inviting them to make the first move. Stampy along with two soldiers approached with caution, while the gnome princess along with a few gnomes approached Stampy.

They met in midway and Stampy decided to break the silence, "Greetings princess, what brings you and your fine company to our borders?" Stampy inquired.

"You are a cat," the princess replied, "I was not expecting to be greeted by a cat. Well, never mind, I and my company are headed this way in search of land and we find our way blocked by you. What do you propose we make of that?"

"You misunderstand our intentions, your majesty; we stand here to ensure that our interests do not conflict with each other," Stampy replied politely.

"What if they do?" the princess replied, "Do you mean to threaten me?"

"No, your majesty; I merely wish to highlight that a conflict is not in the interest of either party," Stampy replied, "I have a proposition from my people that might benefit both of us, should you wish to listen."

"Who are you to determine what is in the interest of me and my clan? I will not trust you to determine our best interest," replied the princess.

Stampy was starting to get annoyed with the princess so he decided to take a different stance than the current one.

"I understand your point of view, but you do not understand that the small group of soldiers is not even a quarter of my army. If it comes to a battle, my soldiers outnumber yours 3 to 1, which means that we may suffer losses but you and your clan face complete annihilation. It is for this reason that I strongly suggest that you hear me out," Stampy stated with a tone of finality.

The princess considered Stampy for a little while as if to consider the truth in his words and then replied, "Very well then, what do you propose we do?"

As soon as she said this, Stampy knew he had won and he narrated his suggestion to her along with the condition. Stampy thought she might change her mind after hearing the condition but she accepted the entire offer and Stampy returned to the village bearing the good news that there was to be no conflict with the gnomes as they had accepted the truce.

Chapter 3:

Gnarly's Betrayal

Stampy and the soldiers, upon their arrival, were greeted by a horde of excited villagers.

"What happened?" cried a voice from the crowd.

"Did they refuse the offer?" someone yelled.

"I knew it. Those good for nothing greedy gnomes want the entire village for themselves," one of the villagers shouted.

"Well that's not going to happen is it? No matter what happens we will not let them set foot in our village."

"Yeah, let them come, we will sort them out."

"This is our village and no one can take it from us."

By this time the entire village was yelling their agreement to the prospect of a battle while Stampy and his soldiers stood there forgotten with annoyed expressions on their faces.

"I told you before, Stampy," said a familiar voice.

"I told you that you should have let me handle them, Stampy! I would have sorted them out in no time, but no worries me and my soldiers can still deal with them," Flash finished enthusiastically, choosing to ignore the raised eyebrows in the crowd. Stampy felt his temper rising at these comments.

"No, when will you people understand that the only way to sort this matter out is for us to present them with my freshly baked cakes. I made this suggestion before the meeting as well, but nobody listens to Lola," Lola protested.

"Why are you so quite, Stampy?" one of the villagers asked realizing that they had not let Stampy speak at all.

"You tried your best, nobody blames you," said another villager sympathetically.

"Yeah, you have nothing to be upset about," replied a third villager. By this time, Stampy and his soldiers had had enough.

"Will you people shut up and let Stampy say something?" yelled one of the soldiers in exasperation.

Finally, everybody fell silent waiting anxiously for Stampy to tell what had happened. Stampy took a long deep breath and said with a satisfied look on his face, "I have just returned from a meeting with the chieftain of the gnomes. I presented her with our planand after much convincing, she finally gave in and accepted it."

The crowd seemed a bit disappointed initially as it seemed that they were actually looking forward to a confrontation with the gnomes. This feeling, however, quickly gave way to the realization that they could go on living peacefully.

The crowd cheered Stampy and was overjoyed that his approach had worked. At this moment, Stampy cleared his throat loudly to get the attention of the crowd and the crowd fell silent.

"I urge you to maintain this peace, which means that you need to put aside these feelings of hostility that you have developed for the gnomes. This does not, however, mean that you let your guard down. We need to be more cautious than ever," warned Stampy.

The crowd seemed perplexed at this warning.

"He wants us to be friendly and skeptical towards the gnomes at the same time?" one of the villagers asked his friend.

Seeing the confusion on the faces of the villagers, Stampy continued:

"The gnomes are a different species altogether with different customs, values and needs. You should know what these customs are and you need to respect them. We need to make sure that our values and their values do not clash. Also, you must make sure that our rules are conveyed to them accurately so that they do not break the rules inadvertently," Stampy finished.

The crowd stood listening intently. Now they were beginning to understand the meaning behind Stampy's carefully phrased words. They clearly understood now that Stampy was telling them to mark their territory clearly so that the gnomes understood who was in charge.

For the next few days, the villagers awaited the arrival of the gnomes. It had been decided to formally welcome them into the forest and emphasize the terms of their stay. As an additional measure it had been decided to take Lola's advice and present the gnomes with cakes as a gesture of good faith.

"Finally you decide to take my advice. You people never learn, do you? Why didn't you accept my advice from the start when you knew that's what you are going to do in the end?" boasted Lola to a very annoyed Flash, when she was told to prepare the cakes on a day's notice.

"I still don't understand why we have to stand in a ceremony to greet these gnomes and present them with cakes," demanded Flash on the day the gnomes were supposed to move in to the forest.

"They might see this as a sign of weakness and the next thing you know they will demand to stay in our village, we cannot have that, Stampy!"

Stampy had been listening to this rant for the past four days and as tired he was of it, he still had to remain calm.

"We have to stand in ceremony for them so that they understand that it is our territory. Also, this will make it easier for them to see our numbers and judge our intentions," explained Stampy.

"That way they will know that we will honor the truce even though we can easily drive them away," Stampy further added in response to Flash's irritable expression.

"As for mistaking it for weakness," continued Stampy, "No gnome can mistake this huge and well trained army to be a sign of weakness," he said, while pointing towards the large line of soldiers that stood behind them at the entrance of the forest.

"I still don't understand why it is necessary," Flash responded stubbornly.

"Wait and watch, you will understand," replied Stampy.

"Oh will you keep quiet," Lola said suddenly, as Flash opened his mouth to continue arguing.

She had been standing idle for a very long time and was itching to become a part of the conversation.

"These gnomes will go head over heels when they taste my cake," said an excited Lola.

"If you people had listened to me before, these gnomes would be walking in as friends and not as a potential cause of worry," she rambled on.

Stampy could not help shaking his head. He had grown tired of these two and just wanted this ceremony to end as quickly as possible.

Suddenly, as if in answer to his prayers, the horn sounded announcing the arrival of the gnomes.

General Flash stiffened at the sound along with his soldiers, standing prepared for any kind of contingency.

"Here they come," stated a wide eyed Lola as the gnome tribe came into view.

They followed the usual routine of slowing down as they sighted the villagers, but this time they formed a single line and approached with the usual caution.

The gnome company stopped at a little distance from Stampy, Flash, and Lola.

The company split from the middle to form two lines and from their midst appeared Gnelissa, their chieftain.

"Welcome my dears, I have been waiting so long for this moment," Lola cried out in excitement just as Gnelissa opened her mouth to say something.

"We haven't really had a chance to meet before. I am Lola, the town's advisor," she explained while hastily moving towards Gnelissa.

"I have a surprise for you and your clan," chirped a speeding Lola with her hands behind her back.

"Lola wait!!" exclaimed Stampy, but Lola, who was in no mood to listen, continued forward.

Meanwhile, there was some visible discomfort within the gnome company. Gnelissa was suddenly stiff and had taken an attack stance, while her soldiers leaped to form a circle around her.

Lola was almost a foot from the gnomes when one of the gnome soldiers placed his sword right at her throat.

"Halt!" he commanded, and Lola stopped dead in her tracks.

She suddenly realized what was happening and her chubby face drained of all color.

On the other hand the General had raised his hand to signal to his troops to get ready.

"Stop!!!" yelled Stampy, "Lola, slowly show what you have in your hands."

Lola muttered, "It's just a cake for the princess, look."

"Nothing dangerous, just a welcome present," Lola explained, "there is plenty for everybody."

Stampy, sensing the tension moved forward holding out his palms to signal that his intentions were to negotiate and not to fight.

Flash commanded a company of soldiers to go with Stampy.

"What is going on?" demanded Stampy in an icy voice, "Lola made her intentions very clear, tell your soldier to let her go."

"Why should I?" replied the gnome princess, "your friend insulted me by speaking first, then she approached me without permission and now you come and command me to let her go."

"You misunderstand our intentions and confuse Lola's excitement with insult and my concern for peace with arrogance. It will, however, do you well if you do not misread my patience as weakness," Stampy stated and turned to look at the soldier nearest to him.

Stampy's soldier jumped up suddenly and kicked the gnome who was holding Lola's hard.

The gnome fell back and Lola was free in an instant. All the gnomes yelled out in protest, but at that moment the entire village army charged forward and encircled the gnomes.

"We came here to welcome you, your highness, not offend you and your people," stated Stampy.

"You and your clan, however, seem to doubt our peace resolve and choose to misinterpret our hospitality," Stampy went on, "now what are we to make of that?"

"Your soldier points his blade at the town advisor and you do not tell your man to stand down even after hearing the explanation; it seems to me as if you were never in the mood to make peace," Stampy said while looking straight at Gnelissa.

"You are surrounded by my men, your majesty, and you can clearly see that they outnumber your clan; it is therefore my advice that you tone down your attitude a bit," said Stampy.

Gnelissa and her gnomes were shocked at the readiness of the army. The gnomes were not prepared for this response. Gnelissa seemed furious over what Stampy had said but she knew that he had the upper hand at the moment.

"We are waiting for your response, your majesty," continued Stampy, "should we finish you off or should we continue with the terms of the truce?" said Stampy making his intentions very clear.

"I believe that we have no option but to continue with the truce," replied Gnelissa.

"A wise choice, your majesty. However, there will be one small change in the terms of our agreement," said Stampy.

"You and your men will not be allowed to take their weapons into the forest. You will have to submit them in the town's armory," Stampy stated.

Gnelissa was beyond herself with rage. She had now realized that this truce involved the surrender of the gnomes.

"Princess, you must understand that your recent actions have sown a seed of distrust between us," Stampy went on, "furthermore, a village can have only one army, and this village already has that."

The gnomes looked defiant; they looked from their princess to Stampy, waiting for the final verdict.

"Tell your soldiers to lay down the weapons, princess," Stampy repeated.

Gnelissa looked straight at Stampy who held her gaze. She knew she had no choice and Stampy could sense that the resolution is near.

"I understand your demands," said Gnelissa, "in order for the truce to prevail, there can be only one army."

"It is, therefore, my decision that in response to your hospitality and as a sign of good faith, we will submit our weapons to your armory for safe keeping," she finished.

The gnomes seemed horrified. It was clear that they did not agree with their princess, however, they had no choice but to accept her decision.

The gnomes started coming forward in groups and placed their weapons on the ground at a little distance from the encircling army of the villagers.

The princess was the last one to come forward, and Stampy, as a sign of respect, collected her sword himself.

"Keep it safe," she said while handing over the weapon, "I will need it back, along with the weapons of my soldiers."

"Don't worry princess, these are your weapons and will not be used by anyone else," assured Stampy.

Stampy had always thought of himself as a cat of his word. He had no intentions of making the gnomes surrender their weapons, but the present event could not be overlooked.

"It's all for the better," Stampy thought to himself, "this way no one will have to worry about the gnomes attacking in the dead of the night."

"Besides, it isn't my fault, they should have let Lola go when she had explained herself," Stampy continued thinking.

"Yes, this is all for the better, we have no intentions of attacking them and now we know that they can't attack us, so it's good now," Stampy reassured himself.

The gnomes had formed lines. Stampy decided that as a friendly gesture he would walk beside Gnelissa and asked her if he could do so.

"If it's alright with you princess, I would like to accompany you to the forest," Stampy asked politely.

Gnelissa looked at him with angry eyes but nodded curtly.

Stampy told his soldiers to sheath their swords.

"There is no danger now," Stampy said, "put your swords away."

The gnomes walked silently with Stampy and his company to the edge of the forest.

"Let it be known to all that the gnomes have graciously accepted the truce," Stampy declared.

"They will continue to live in our forest as our allies under our protection and governed by the rules of our village," Stampy concluded.

"As a token of our friendship I offer them this package of cakes prepared for them by the villagers to symbolize the bond we will share," Stampy said while presenting the cakes to the gnomes.

"Let us now proceed to the forest where our guests will reside for as long as they wish," stated Stampy.

The company marched forward into the forests; however, they all understood that the gnomes would retaliate at the first opportunity.

Stampy stopped when he reached the heart of the forest.

"You will find this place more to your liking, your majesty," Stampy explained.

"It is very close to the village and the soldiers patrol nearby, which will make it easier for us to remain in contact," Stampy went on.

After addressing the princess, Stampy turned to the rest of the gnome, "You are our guests and we welcome you in our forest for as long as you wish. However, there are certain matters which you need to understand."

"Your safety is the responsibility of the village, which is why a battalion of soldiers, specially maintained for your security, will serve you as the night guard and will be replaced by a fresh battalion in the morning."

"If you have anything to discuss or any complaint, you will have to inform the Captain of the guards who will deliver the message to the village council and we will come and discuss it with you."

"The gnomes and their princess are free to leave the forest whenever they please at which point your weapons will be returned to you."

"You are welcome to stay here for as long as you wish, however, during your stay the laws of the village of Tuk Tuk will bind you."

"All disputes and issues that may arise among the gnomes will be dealt with according to the village laws."

"During your stay in the forest your health will be the responsibility of the village authorities in the same manner as the rest of the village people."

"Lastly, you must adhere to the truce at all times, according to which the gnomes will reside in the forest and can be visited by the villagers occasionally. But the gnomes will not extend their reach to the village and will only visit with prior consent of the villagers."

"These regulations are in place to maintain peace, for our mutual benefit. I hope our guests will not misunderstand our intentions as nothing would please us more than to extend our hospitality to you."

"Having established the norms and conditions of this truce, I must urge my guests to get some rest for now, as the villagers are preparing a feast in your honor," Stampy concluded.

The gnomes and their princess were listening intently to every word Stampy said, and they had understood they were completely at the mercy of the villagers.

It was difficult for them to understand if the villagers were friends or foe, however, for now they had no choice but to think of them as potential enemies.

They greatly disliked Stampy and hated the fact that he had so much power over them. These gnomes were in no mood to forget the humiliation they had suffered from the hands of Stampy and the villagers. Furthermore, the gnomes thought that the rules that Stampy had just laid out meant that the villagers were holding them as prisoners.

The truth was that the gnomes did intend to take over the village eventually and these measures taken by the villagers served to strengthen their resolve. It would obviously be difficult without the weapons, but it was not impossible.

Gnelissa and the gnomes stood and watched Stampy and his soldiers depart.

She knew that her people were furious with her. She knew that if she didn't come up with a quick solution it might lead to a revolt against her.

Stampy's company was far from sight now and there was silence in the gnome camp. Gnelissa knew that this silence had to be broken somehow.

"My fellow gnomes, I understand that this treatment from the villagers has made you angry," she started.

"But you must understand that this is not the end. Eventually we will find a way to avenge this humiliation, however, for now we must honor the truce."

"These villagers may have insulted us but still they have provided us with a place to stay and there is a good chance that they may keep their end of the bargain."

"I think we should give them a chance to prove their sincerity. I think a truce might just work out and we might get along with the villagers. They seem to be honest and hardworking folk who just want to keep what is rightfully theirs. They viewed us as a potential threat and our rash actions convinced them of this. I believe their reaction was natural, it is just what we would have done if someone threatened us."

"These villagers still intend to extend their hospitality to us, which means that they have every intention of handling this matter peacefully."

"I know you are angry right now but if you think about it, the villagers have proven to be very generous. They have agreed to share their land with a group of homeless gnomes."

"We finally have a place which we might learn to call our home; all we have to do is cooperate a little."

"I urge you to not let your temper get the better of you, think about what we stand to gain from this truce and don't jump to rash conclusions," explained Gnelissa.

Gnelissa's speech seemed to make sense to many gnomes. The expressions of many had softened and many nodded their approval at her words. The realization started to dawn on them that these villagers had actually reacted in self defense and nothing else.

It seemed that Gnelissa had almost every gnome convinced to give this truce a chance; however, there was a small group of cynical gnomes which were not convinced at all. This group of gnomes was led by a huge gnome called Gnarly. Gnarly was the son of a former chief of the gnomes. His father had been the chief before Gnelissa's father. Gnarly was very young when his father passed away, and his father's most trusted advisor and best friend was made the chief instead. The new chief was Gnelissa's father who was much loved by all gnomes. When he passed away, Gnarly was of age and so was Gnelissa. However, Gnarly was a bully and people didn't like him much. On the other hand, everyone adored Gnelissa which was why she was made the princess of the gnomes.

This did not go well with Gnarly who viewed Gnelissa and her father as usurpers, and held a grudge against them.

Gnarly and his goons were also amongst the crowd when Gnelissa was making her speech. He did not want this truce to continue as he viewed this as the only way to get rid of Gnelissa.

"Well, isn't that touching, it seems as if our princess developed a soft corner for the villagers," came the voice of Gnarly.

"It seems that these villagers have two leaders looking after their interests. One is that cat and the other one is our very own princess."

"Are you accusing me of treason, Gnarly?" Gnelissa asked in a daring voice.

"So what if I am?" replied Gnarly.

All the gnomes seemed angry at this accusation.

"Hold your tongue Gnarly," there came a voice from the crowd.

"You are talking about our princess. How dare you accuse her of this?" asked someone from the crowd.

"You must not speak to the princess in this manner," a third person said.

"Why shouldn't I?" Gnarly asked, "according to her, everything is our fault."

"We approached them in a hostile manner, while they were extremely peaceful."

"We were the ones who acted in a rash manner, while the village people embarrassed us, again in self-defense," continued Gnarly sarcastically.

"Whose side are you on, your majesty?" asked Gnarly.

"Why don't you people understand that this is a trick of theirs? Soon they will turn us into their slaves. Will you people realize then?" Gnarly went on.

"These villagers have taken away all your weapons, which means you cannot fight them."

"They have surrounded you with their army so that they can attack you at the right time."

"They have imposed their rules upon you like they are your masters and you still think that these people intend to be our friends."

"My dear friends, it is high time that you wake up. They intend to impose their dominance on us and we must resist it."

"Don't you see what's happening? That cat is trying to rule us. Where is your honor? Are the gnomes prepared to live under the rule of a cat?" Gnarly finished.

"NOOOOO!" Exclaimed a vast majority.

Gnelissa was standing there listening to Gnarly. She quietly watched as he poisoned the hearts of all her people with his venomous words. She could hear their cries of hate and see the hatred in their eyes. Within seconds they had lost all sense and this did not settle well with her.

"ENOUGH!" Gnelissa yelled out in a loud clear voice.

"I will not have you disregard my decision, Gnarly. I am the princess of this clan and you are bound by honor to respect my decision; you all are, for that matter."

"There is no higher honor than following the decision of the princess - that's the gnome law and you will abide by it," established an angry Gnelissa.

"Gnome law? As far as I can recall we are bound by the law of Tuk Tuk army, princess," said Gnarly taking a few steps towards Gnelissa.

"Gnome Law does not apply to us here, thanks to you," Ganrly said.

"No gnome princess could abandon the gnome law like Gnelissa did; I hereby claim this tribe and banish…."

"Hold your tongue boy," interrupted an old gnome.

"You have no claim to rule the clan, Gnarly, by any prevailing law," he continued.

"Gnomes laws were established by our forefathers and they define us. You are not a gnome if you don't follow these laws."

"It clearly stated in the gnome laws that gnomes are to respect the laws of all other beings while living amongst them, even cats, but their personal life will always be governed by these laws."

"These laws also state that any gnome who causes hindrance or challenges the authority of the chief, except to uphold the gnome law, will be treated as a traitor and will be banished from the clan," the old gnome concluded.

The impact of these words was significant. Every eye was on Gnarly, as if daring him to repeat his claim. Gnelissa's authority had been re-established in an absolute manner. No gnome could question her decision now.

"What do you propose we do now, Gnarly?" Gnelissa asked.

"Do you wish to leave the clan?" she asked Gnarly.

"No, your majesty," Gnarly replied.

"Then as long as I am alive, you will follow my command, and that goes for all gnomes in this clan."

"You will respect my decisions and abide by them," Gnelissa said furiously.

"Now we must take some rest; we have wasted a lot of time already and it's almost nightfall, we must be fresh for the feast," she concluded.

All the gnomes followed suit for no one wished to anger Gnelissa any further. They all knew that the next one to disobey her would be banished for sure.

Gnelissa's authority was clear for everyone except Gnarly.

"Until next time princess," he said quietly so that only his friends could hear him.

"You will have to do something about him, princess," advised the old gnome.

"I most certainly will, book keeper," replied Gnelissa.

Meanwhile, Stampy, Flash and Lola were marching with the army towards the village.

"I wasn't expecting them to be this mean," said a hysterical Lola.

Lola hadn't recovered from that incident as yet. She couldn't believe that the gnomes had actually tried to kill her even when she had worked so hard to bake all those cakes for them.

"All that time I put in to baking those wonderful cakes for them and this is what I get," said Lola.

"I hate gnomes. Flash, you were right, we should have killed them when we had the chance. These creatures do not deserve our hospitality," she concluded.

"Will you stop crying about it already? It was your fault in the first place. Why did you have to run towards their chief?" Flash responded.

"That too with your hands behind you, as if you were carrying a knife to stab the princess," Flash continued.

"What did you think they would do to you? Hug you, accept your cake, eat it, thank you, and then let you go?"

"You are lucky to be alive, Lola," Flash concluded.

"Oh yes, it's my fault that I tried to intervene and be nice to them. They were complete angels to point their swords at me and hold me hostage."

"I was very excited to finally meet them so I rushed to greet them. If I had only known that they would be this rude I would never have tried," Lola replied.

"It's no use explaining anything to you because will never admit your mistake," said an irritated Flash.

"What do you think, Stampy? Do you also believe that it's my fault?" asked Lola innocently.

Stampy had remained silent this whole time. The day's events had not turned out as he had planned. Making the gnomes surrender was not what he wanted, but believed that it was a good measure altogether. Despite all this he was annoyed with Lola; he couldn't make sense of her actions but then again she meant no harm. She was only trying to be nice and the gnomes should have let her go when they discovered the cake in her hands. What did their actions signify? Were they here to take the village by force? Was that their intention even after agreeing to the truce? What will they do now? Will they live peacefully or will they make mischief? These were the questions bothering Stampy when he heard Lola.

"I don't blame you, Lola, your intentions were good," Stampy replied after much thought.

"Nonetheless, you shouldn't have approached the gnomes the way you did," Stampy added.

"But why don't you understand that I was excited to see them?" said a hopping Lola, "you people blame me for everything."

"We understand that fully Lola," replied an irritated Stampy with a raised voice, "What you don't understand is that your excitement could have ended in a war, and would have resulted in a never ending hatred between the village people and the gnomes. Do you want that?"

"No, I never want something so horrible for anyone," replied Lola, "I just didn't see it that way, I…."

"We understand that you didn't do it on purpose," interrupted Stampy, "but you must understand the seriousness of your actions."

"I do," replied Lola.

"Then that's all that matters," Stampy replied politely, "forget about it as it turned out just fine."

"Now I need you to do me a favor, Lola. Please inform all the Captains of the army to meet me in the village hall to discuss the matter of the gnomes," Stampy told Lola.

"The General will come with me," Stampy said turning towards the pony carrying Flash.

Bill, the pony, was Flash's close and most trusted companion. He was a proud animal who would only let the General sit on his back on all important occasions.

Lola had flown ahead to inform the Captains just as the army had turned towards their barracks, while Bill and Flash went straight towards the village hall with Stampy.

The soldiers were ordered to make their way towards their barracks, whereas, the Captains followed Stampy and Flash.

Lola had flown to her little bakery to prepare refreshments for everyone. This was one of the great things about Lola - she understood what was expected of her.

In just a short while, Stampy, Flash with Bill, and the Captains were all assembled in the village hall.

"Today's events didn't go as planned," Stampy started by stating the obvious.

"Nonetheless, everything turned out in our favor," Stampy continued, "the surrender of the gnomes is a big achievement for us."
All the Captains nodded in approval.

"We don't have to remain cautious against the gnomes. This, however, doesn't mean that we can let our guard down."

"We need to make these gnomes feel welcome and at home; the slightest mistake on our part could end up in a disaster as they are significant in number and a potential threat even without weapons."

All the Captains were listening to Stampy; they could understand the seriousness of the matter from his tone.

"We have promised to provide them security and look after their needs and that is exactly what we need to do."

"I know that you do not like the gnomes much and I understand that they don't intend to make things easy for us; however, as hosts we have to act as the better people."

"I want you, along with all your soldiers, to be vigilant at all times. You must be sure to avoid any trouble with the gnomes and they need to be treated in the same way as you would treat the villagers."

"Remember, as we have taken them into our protection, they need to be treated like we treat our people."

"These gnomes did not come for truce today; I have a feeling that they had something else in mind, but we succeeded in crushing those intentions today."

"However, they will not take this lightly. We have taken away their weapons and have imposed our rules upon them. I will be surprised if they aren't brewing something as we speak."

"This brings me to tonight's feast. I want the soldiers to be vigilant at all times and to be prepared for anything."

"That has been taken care of, Stampy," interrupted Flash.

"I have prepared a team of my best soldiers to be present at the feast without uniform. These soldiers will be present among the crowd to respond quickly to any unfortunate event."

"There will be an outer circle of soldiers standing guard surrounding the area. These soldiers, however, will be present at a little distance from the crowd, hidden from view."

"The major chunk of the army will be on alert to respond at a minutes' notice," established Flash.

Stampy stood there listening to Flash. He did not know that Flash was capable of such plans. Flash had accounted for all contingencies in his plan and that was very impressive.

"Well, he is the General for a reason," Stampy thought to himself.

"That sounds quite impressive, General, you have planned for almost everything," Stampy said out loud.

Flash was beaming with pride at Stampy's comment.

"I believe this will be all for today, you all can now leave to make all necessary arrangements," Flash said dismissing the Captains.

The Captains left hurriedly, realizing that they had a lot to do in very little time.

"I have a feeling that the feast will go peacefully without any unpleasant surprises," Stampy told Flash voicing his satisfaction at the arrangements.

Just at that moment Lola arrived in the hall carrying plenty of dishes with refreshments.

"It isn't much but that's all I could do at such a short notice," she started.

"You know, Stampy, you could have told me beforehand about this meeting. That way I would have prepared something better for everyone, but, well, you planned this at the last moment yourself soo......"

"Hey, where did everybody go?"

She looked at Stampy and Flash and realized that everybody had left.

"Well isn't that just great! Everybody left, but did anybody bother telling me about it? No, because, you people, were too busy talking about the important stuff; besides who cares about Lola? You can give her all the work and not bother telling her when everyone has left."

"Well, this is just it! I have had it with the two of you. I have to do so much work but instead of being appreciated, I get ignored."

"Oh will you stop whining!" cried an annoyed Flash, "we did not do it on purpose"

"It's just that the refreshments didn't arrive by the time the meeting ended so they all left."

"Also, in case you didn't notice, I, Stampy and Bill are still here, and we are starving. So instead of going on one of your tantrums, you can serve the refreshments and join us for a snack," finished Flash.

"Oh I am so sorry," Lola responded, "I didn't realize that you guys were starving, come to think of it I haven't eaten anything in a while and…..."

"You just had a cake all to yourself when we were in the forest and Stampy was explaining everything to the gnomes," interrupted Flash.

"That was an hour ago," snapped Lola, "and considering the amount of work I have done since then, I believe I deserve a snack."

"Yeah yeah, you and your hourly snacks, no wonder you can't lose weight," Flash retorted.

"Can we please eat?" Stampy intervened, before Lola could respond.

Stampy was growing weary of them having a go at each other. It was too much, plus he had lot on his mind and he wanted to think.

"Sure we can," replied Lola giving Flash a furious look.

They finished their refreshments and headed to their respective destinations to get ready for the feast. Before going back to his place Stampy headed to the village market to check how the arrangements were coming along. To his surprise, everything was almost done and the last of the chairs were being set up. Stampy was pleased to see this and headed back to his house to get some rest before the feast.

While over at the gnome camp most of the gnomes were resting, Gnelissa and Gnarly could not help but think about the day's events.

Gnelissa was recalling the day's events, while lounging in her tent, which the gnomes had set up as a top priority.

She had to surrender to Stampy and then she had her authority challenged by that oaf Gnarly. She couldn't decide which one to treat as a more serious threat. She wasn't expecting Gnarly to challenge her like this, at a time when the gnomes were facing a potential threat.

"Potential threat?" she thought to herself, "the villagers do not seem to be in any mood to go back on their word. I think they won't do anything to harm us, unless they are provoked."

"I need to believe in what I told my people, the villagers are generous and they deserve our trust. But have we earned theirs'?"

"The assault on that bird, whatever her name is, was very serious. I need to amend that at the first opportunity I get."

"It won't be easy but I still have to try."

"Meanwhile, what should I do about Gnarly? He has made his intentions very clear. He wants to be chief and he will use any means to achieve this. He will use any situation to his advantage but I need to make sure that he doesn't get another opportunity."

"He almost had everybody convinced today, but bless that old book keeper for if it wasn't for him, I wouldn't be a princess anymore."

"It is decided. I need to befriend the villagers and find a way to punish Gnarly."

"Well, punishing him won't be too difficult; he is bound to present an opportunity now and then and when he does he will be sorry," the princess seemed to be content at that thought and finally closed her eyes to rest.

On the other hand Gnarly was fuming over the missed opportunity and his goons were on the receiving end of it.

"So close, so close, and that old book keeper had to poke his nose to defend that princess," he yelled angrily, "I will have to teach him a lesson that he never forgets."

"I have to be careful from now on, that Gnelissa will be on the lookout for any mistake I make to have me banished," said Gnarly, talking more to himself than anyone else, while his friends were watching not knowing what to say or do.

"They turned against me in an instant when he spoke," Gnarly went on, "I will get him for this I tell you."

"But I need to sort the princess out first, but she is much stronger now with the support of all the gnomes and the villagers. They would not allow a change in leadership at this time."

"The gnomes are on their way to befriend the villagers who would accept their friendship easily, which would strengthen Gnelissa even further."

"I can't let this happen, I have to find a way to drive a wedge between the gnomes and the villagers, but how?"

"They won't listen to me anymore; they only listen to their precious princess as she is the key to them having a new home and new friends."

"If only she wasn't around I could…," Gnarly stopped in mid sentence, and his look changed from worried to excitement.

"If she wasn't around all my worries would be gone, and I can blame it on the villagers, which will cause the gnomes to hate them."

"But how are you going to get rid of her Gnarly?" one of his friends finally plucked up the courage to ask.

"Me? No, we are going to kidnap her and blame her disappearance on the villagers," Gnarly replied.

"But that won't make the villagers hate the gnomes," said another one of Gnarly's friends, "I mean the villagers need to hate the gnomes as well, don't you think?"

"I sure do my friend, that's why we are going to kidnap someone from their side as well," Gnarly replied.

"You mean kidnap a villager?" his friend asked, "do you have someone in mind?"

"Oh yes," gnarly responded.

"Who is it?" the friend asked.

"The bird that was assaulted today for approaching without permission," Gnarly replied with an evil grin.

The time for the feast had arrived and the gnomes were waiting for their princess to leave her tent. The gnomes were confused as to their manner of approach.

"Will we have to wait for them to formally escort us into the village?" asked one of the gnomes

"I believe so; we don't want to give them a reason to panic," replied his friend, "besides, we wouldn't like it if some guest just barged into our camp, would we?"

"You are right, let's wait for them," replied the first gnome.

"But wouldn't that seem too proud?" asked an old gnome, "I mean they have already invited us. I believe they would expect us to come on our own."

"I think we should proceed towards the village," commented a fourth gnome.

These comments had started quite an argument among the gnomes.

"What is meaning of this?" she demanded.

"What are you arguing about?" she continued.

"They are deciding whether they should approach the village or should they wait for some sign from the villagers," the book keeper responded to the princess's question.

"Hmmm, I was thinking about it myself and I believe that it will be wise to wait a little while for some sign from the villagers," she said.

As soon as she said that, there was a loud sound announcing the arrival of the village guard. They were a company of about twenty hares, all clad in full armor. One of them moved forward to the center of the gnome camp towards the princess.

"Your majesty, we are here representing the villagers and we are here to escort you and your people to the village feast," the soldier made the announcement and stepped away and resumed his position in front of the soldiers.

At this point the princess stepped forward and the soldiers formed ranks on either side creating a wide passage for Gnelissa and her company.

The gnomes moved forward, and after covering a little distance, they realized that the entire passage leading to the village had been lined with soldiers in anticipation of their arrival.

At the very entrance of the gate, stood Stampy, Lola and Flash mounted on Bill.

"Welcome, princess, I hope you are well rested and in good health," greeted Stampy cheerfully when the princess approached.

"Please come in, we have a wonderful feast prepared for you and your people," he concluded.

Having exchanged the usual greetings, Stampy along with Lola and Flash, led the princess and gnomes towards the feast.

Gnelissa had chosen to walk beside Lola who seemed a bit uncomfortable with that.

"Hello," Gnelissa said to Lola.

"Hello," Lola replied nervously.

"I am really sorry about what happened in the morning," Gnelissa started, "it was not our intention to cause any trouble."

"Hmmm," Lola responded.

Gnelissa realized that the memory was, perhaps, still fresh in Lola's mind so she decided to let it go for the moment.

Stampy had overheard the conversation and he was mildly pleased with the fact that although Gnelissa was trying to make an effort towards Lola, Lola was not responding well to it. He felt the need to talk to Lola about taking it easy with the gnomes.

"Right this way princess," Stampy said leading the company towards the feast.

It was all very well organized. The village market was decorated with multiple lanterns with the corners lined with tables bearing all kinds of tasty food.

The gnomes seemed impressed.

"You seemed to have made quite some arrangements," commented Gnelissa.

"We were planning it for a few days, princess," replied Stampy.

The villagers were taking the lead in inviting their guests to enjoy the festivities. The gnomes seemed a bit shy but the villagers were making sure that the gnomes enjoyed themselves.

It took them a little while but the gnomes had started laughing and talking with the villagers, while enjoying the food.

Lola's cakes seemed to be the highlight of the feast. She was beaming at the amount of complements she was getting.

"You have cooked them beautifully," commented an elderly Gnome, "I haven't tasted such amazing cakes in my entire life."

"You are too kind," replied an excited Lola.

"I can't stop eating, even though I am full," commented another gnome.

"Pleased have some more then," Lola said.

"You must send us more of these cakes of yours," said a third gnome.

"I most definitely will," said Lola while hopping slightly.

Gnelissa realized that it was the perfect opportunity to make things right with Lola.

"The cakes were delicious Lola," Gnelissa said.

"Oh you must st…," Lola stopped in mid sentence when she realized who she was talking to.

The change in her tone and expressions was drastic.

"Oh well, thank you then," she responded coldly to Gnelissa's compliment and walked away.

Stampy, who was standing nearby, decided that enough is enough and he followed Lola to talk to her.

"Lola, wait!" he yelled.

"Why, what is it, Stampy? Are you here to complement me on my cakes as well?" Lola asked.

"No, Lola, I am here to make you understand that the way you are behaving with the princess is not cool," Stampy told her.

"What do you mean, Stampy?" Lola asked, "do you want me to be best friends with the person who tried to kill me?"

"We have discussed this Lola," stampy replied through gritted teeth, "it was your fault as well and even if it wasn't, they have paid the price for this mistake. It is, therefore, I suggest that you make peace with Gnelissa."

"Especially when she is trying to make things right with you," Stampy concluded.

Lola looked rebellious at this aspect, so Stampy tried to take a different tone with her.

"You must understand, Lola, that this is bigger than any one individual, it is very crucial to the interest of the villagers," Stampy explained.

"You must throw aside your grudge against her and the gnomes, and remember that it was you who wanted us to be friends with the gnomes in the first place," Stampy reminded her.

"You must stop being angry with Gnelissa, she has already apologized to you and I think you should forgive her."

These statements subdued Lola somewhat.

"Alright, if you think that this is really in the interest of the villagers," Lola replied, "then I will do it."

"Thank you Lola," Stampy responded with a sigh of relief.

"Now please go to the princess and sort things out," Stampy told Lola.

Although Lola did not like this one bit, she still grudgingly approached Gnelissa.

"Gnelissa," Lola called out.

"Yes, Lola?" Gnelissa replied.

"I believe we got off on the wrong foot," Lola began.

"I do believe that we should start fresh just like you said," she continued.

"I am glad you feel this way Lola," said a happy Gnelissa.

"Well, I see the two of you are getting along well," interrupted Stampy.

"Yes we are, as a matter of fact, Lola and I have decided to put the past behind us," declared Gnelissa.

"All in the interest of our people," she said.

"I see this as a beginning of a new era," she continued, "it seems that our people will get along just fine."

"I certainly hope so," replied Stampy.

"I think we will be just fine," said an optimistic Lola.

On the other hand, Gnarly had a different thought as to how things would turn out. He was eyeing the three of them from the very beginning.

"We need to execute our plan tonight only," Gnarly told his friends.

"We can't let this friendship blossom; we need to crush it while it is still fresh," he continued.

"Gash, did you scout the area as I told you to?" Gnarly barked at one of his accomplices.

"I did, Gnarly; the area is creeping with soldiers. We will have to be very careful," Gash replied.

"I know about the soldiers, you fool. You were supposed to look for loop holes in the security," Gnarly yelled at him, "do I have to do everything myself?"

"That's what I am trying to tell you, Gnarly, the forest is fortified, and the only place where there are no guards is the village hall right across the market but we can't go there," Gash replied.

Gnarly smiled.

"It seems the odds are on our side today. If the princess goes missing from the village then our plan will work out just fine," Gnarly replied.

"But they will start searching for her right away and this will not give us much time to escape," Gash pointed out.

"Don't you think I know that already?" Gnarly responded, "but this is as good an opportunity as we will ever get to rid ourselves of the princess."

"Which means that you and your gnomes will have to make haste," continued Gnarly.

"Do you understand?" he asked in a threatening way.

"Yes, Gnarly, I do, but how will we kidnap her and then how will we sneak her out of here?" Gash asked.

"You and your gnomes will have to go and hide at the hall while I will lead Gnelissa there," Gnarly explained.

"As soon as she gets there, you will hit her on the head to make her unconscious, but be careful. Do not hit her too hard or she might die."

"As soon as she loses her consciousness, you will take her out through the back of the village to the riverside. They won't have anyone guarding that side as they have everybody stationed towards the gnome camp."

"You will have to take her outside of the village and then kill her at the first opportunity you get. Then you will make your way back to the camp," Gnarly concluded.

"Why don't we kill her in the hall? That will prove that the villagers killed her," Gash asked.

"Why do you even try to use your brain?" Gnarly asked rhetorically.

"You fool! No villager will kill her and leave her body in the village, now shut up and do as you are told," he yelled.

"Ok, I was only trying to help," Gash replied.

"LEAVEEEE!!" screamed Gnarly.

"Ok, Ok I am leaving," Gash said while moving away from Gnarly.

"Go straight to the hall along with your gnomes and make sure no one sees you," Gnarly commanded Gash just as he left.

Gnarly's eyes were fixed on the princess; he waited for a while and then started to walk towards the city hall. He made sure that no one saw him except for the princess.

Meanwhile, the princess saw Gnarly walking away from the festival and making his way further into the village. Something did not seem right to her.

"Please excuse me, I will be right back," she told Stampy and started following Gnarly as quietly as possible.

She realized that Gnarly was in fact going towards the village hall. She followed him and saw him disappear into the building.

She was torn between telling the village authority about Gnarly's suspicious behavior and following him inside the hall to check what he is up to, and after much thought she finally decided to go in after him.

The inside of the hall was dark and she couldn't see anything.

"Gnarly, I know you are in here, I saw you walk inside. Now come on out and stop whatever mischief you…"

Just then something hit her hard on the head and she fell unconscious.

"Well done boys, now take her away quickly before any one sees us and do as I told you. We will meet back at the camp," Gnarly told his men and hurriedly left the building making his way towards the market.

He knew for a fact that nobody had seen him, because everybody was busy with the feast. He looked over at Stampy, Lola and Flash and he saw that they were still busy talking to each other.

Nobody could stop him from becoming the chief of gnomes and nobody would be able to stop him from taking over this village. All he had to do now was to wait for everyone to realize that the princess was missing. Then everything would fall into place.

It was just before the gnomes were about to leave that everyone realized that the princess was missing.

"Where is Gnelissa?" Stampy asked.

"It's been quite a while now and she hasn't come back," Stampy continued.

"She went into the crowd. I will go and look for her," Lola replied.

"Please do, everyone is about to leave," Stampy told Lola.

Stampy wanted to address the crowd alongside Gnelissa as, according to him, that would send a good message to the people.

Lola hurried into the crowd to look for Gnelissa. After looking around for a while she decided to ask the gnomes if they had seen her.

"Hey, have you seen the princess?" she asked a gnome.

"No, I haven't, ma'am," the gnome replied.

She continued to question everyone, until she came across Gnarly who had mischief up his sleeve.

"What do you mean by asking me about the princess's whereabouts. I haven't seen her since she was standing over there with you and Stampy," he replied, rather loudly so that everyone could hear, pointing to the place where Stampy and Flash were standing.

"Do you mean to say that our princess is missing?" Gnarly asked loudly.

The crowd was silent now. Everybody had realized that something had gone wrong. They were all looking at Lola, who was standing right in the midst of a large gnome company.

Stampy could sense the sudden hostility in the gnome crowd and he signaled to a soldier clad in plain clothes to go and help Lola.

"Why are you so quite? Where is our princess?" asked the gnome closest to Lola.

"I-I don..," Lola had only begun to respond before a gnome cut in.

"Is she alright?"

"Of course she is, wha..," again a gnome interrupted her.

"Then where is she? Why won't you tell us where she is?"

The gnomes were closing in on her.

"What have you people done with her?" asked one of the gnomes.

"Have you killed her?" a gnome asked, completely losing his head.

"Noo, we would never do that," Lola replied.

"Then where is she?" Gnarly asked loudly, "is this your way of avenging the morning's incident?"

"Was this your plan that you invite us for a feast to kill our princess?"

"No no, I don't know what you people are talking about," Lola responded hysterically.

"LIAARRRR!!" a gnome cried out and leapt at her.

Just then a few guards jumped in with their swords pulled out, one of whom kicked the leaping gnome.

"Stand back," the leader of the group warned the gnomes.

But the gnomes seemed rebellious; it seemed that they viewed every villager as an enemy. A riot was about to break out. The soldiers, however, were prepared and sensing the mood they decided to show themselves by drawing out their swords. The gnomes were not expecting soldiers among the crowd and were taken aback by this response.

"You see, do you see now what these villagers think of you," Gnarly cried out addressing the gnomes.

"This is the level of their trust. They have soldiers hidden among the crowd. Is this how you welcome your guests?"

"You must open your eyes now, my people, these villagers do not think of you as friends. If they did, they wouldn't have felt the need to welcome us with soldiers."

"In fact I don't think that it's a coincidence that our princess has gone missing and the villagers have their soldiers prepared to handle a possible riot."

"It was all properly planned if you ask me. These people had planned to harm the princess and tackle us by means of their army," Gnarly shouted.

"That will be enough," Flash told Gnarly in a loud clear voice.

"I am the General of this village and its security is my responsibility."

"It is true that your princess can not be found at the moment, however, that does not imply that something bad has happened to her."

"Then what does it imply, General?" Gnarly asked in a mocking tone, "where is the princess?"

"We don't know where she is, but we are looking for her, just like you," Flash replied.

"Right now the best way to help your princess is to stop this racket and let us look for her with peace," Flash continued.

"The gnomes are welcome to help us search for her if they want. But please do not make things more difficult for us, because if things get any worse we will be compelled to use force against you," Flash warned.

"Are you threatening us, General?" Gnarly asked.

"No, I am just stating the facts. Now if you stay quiet for a while, we might get to important matters," Flash snapped.

"I am talking to all the gnomes present here at the moment. Do you really think that a riot will help your princess? If you really want to help her I advise you join hands with us."

The crowd fell silent.

"Now do we have any gnome volunteers for the search?" Flash asked.

"We will help," the book keeper replied stepping forward with a few gnomes.

"We will help look for the princess," repeated the book keeper. "So be it," Flash said.

Meanwhile Gash and his gnomes were carrying the princess out of the village to the riverside. One of the gnomes had the princess on his back; they were taking turns to carry her.

"Wait, this is as good a place as any, put her down here," Gash commanded.

The Gnome carrying the princess put her down on the ground.

"Now go get a heavy stone, all of you," Gash ordered for a second time, "and let's be done with it."

The gnomes dispersed in search for a heavy stone, while Gash stood guarding the princess.

The princess began to stir but Gash didn't notice as he had his back towards her.

"Will you hurry up?" Gash barked after the other gnomes, "we need don't have much time, if the villagers find us next to her dead body or if any one catches us in the act, we will have a heavy price to pay."

The princess suddenly realized what was happening, her head was bursting from the blow that got her unconscious, but she had enough wits about her to focus on what she needed to do.

She realized from what Gash had said, that there were other gnomes in the vicinity who wanted her dead, but they were not present here at the moment. She knew she had to act now.

Frantically thinking of what to do, she noticed a thick piece of wood, placed at a little distance from where she was. She got up quietly and slowly, picked up the piece of wood and slammed it over Gash's head.

He fell to the ground, unconscious. The princess, taking advantage of this opportunity, ran towards the forest. She didn't know where she was going or where the village was, all she knew was that she had to run away from this place.

She kept running and running till she tripped over a tree root. She fell to the ground, which brought her to her senses. Panting for breath she noticed that she was deep into the forest and it was very dark. She looked back from the way she came and saw that no one was chasing her. She didn't know what to do, except that she couldn't continue running into the forest.

"What should I do? What Should I do?" she kept asking herself.

"If I continue to run into the forest, I might get lost, but if I go back I might get killed."

"But getting lost won't help me much either," she reasoned with herself.

"I need to go back to the village."

"But I need to be very careful, I can't risk getting caught," she decided finally.

Very carefully, Gnelissa started tracing her footsteps back to where she had come from.

She kept walking, hoping all the while that she had taken the right way, and suddenly she heard some gnomes talking to each other. She couldn't make out what they were saying so she decided to move a bit closer.

"….think he is dead," she heard a Gnome say.

"How did this happen? We were away for only a little while," another gnome was saying.

"Isn't it obvious? The princess must have woken up, realized what was happening, and decided to run, while killing Gash on the way," the first gnome explained.

By this time the princess had moved a bit more closer in order to see the gnomes clearly.

"What should we do now?" asked the second gnome.

"I believe that we should make our way back to the camp and consult with Gnarly. He will know what to do," replied the first gnome.

"You are right but what do we do with Gash, leave him here?" the second gnome asked.

"There isn't anything that we can do, can we? I think leaving him here would be the right thing to do," the first gnome replied.

"Ok let's go," the second gnome agreed and they went off at a quick pace.

The princess realized that this was her only chance of getting back so she started following them carefully. All the while she was thinking of the treason that Gnarly had committed and was cursing herself for not punishing him when she had a chance.

"I will teach him a lesson he will not forget easy, once I get back," she thought to herself.

She was following them as carefully as possible, all the while hoping that they didn't realize that they were being followed.

The gnomes were moving at a great pace but suddenly they slowed down. Gnelissa realized that this caution was due to the sounds coming from the village and her spirits rose. All she could think now was to reach the camp as quickly as possible.

The gnomes had quickened their pace again and were heading straight to the camp. Gnelissa continued to follow them from a distance. She knew all her worries were about to vanish, her people would take care of everything.

This happiness soon disappeared from her mind when she saw the camp was empty.

"Well freedom is only a little way away, I guess I will have to wait it out," Gnelissa thought to herself.

Chapter 4:

All's Well that Ends Well

The village was in an uproar. The gnomes were angry as they couldn't find their princess and the villagers were angry and disappointed at the attitude of the gnomes. Lola was upset but she concealed it well. She knew that everybody was really worried at the moment so she kept her problems to herself.

Stampy, on the other hand, was very angry. He was upset with Gnelissa for disappearing like this, whatever her reason maybe and he was frustrated at the behavior of the gnomes who had tried to attack Lola for the second time that day.

Stampy was very happy with Flash, as he was handling the matter very well, but Stampy knew that even Flash was frustrated with the gnomes.

Flash was leading a company of soldiers to search for the princess in the village, and he had sent out numerous others in various directions to look for her. Flash's faithful friend Bill was with him at all times and was pacing up and down the village with Flash on his back.

The book keeper and his company were with Flash.

"What do they call you?" Flash asked him.

"The book keeper," replied the old Gnome.

"That is a strange name," Flash commented.

"It is more of a title than a name. I am the bearer of the ancient law book of gnomes. I have been called by this title for a long time now."

"Well all right then book keeper, tell me who that giant Gnome is, the one who was instigating your people?" Flash asked.

"That is Gnarly, the son of the gnome chief who was the predecessor of Gnelissa's father," the book keeper replied.

"How are his terms with the princess?" Flash asked.

"Not very good I'm afraid, he tried to overthrow Gnelissa right after you people left our camp," the book keeper continued.

"He doesn't like the princess much; he thinks that she and her father usurped his throne, which is not true, of course, because Gnelissa's father was asked to take the throne by Gnarly's father. Gnarly was too young to rule at that time."

"That can qualify as a motive to kidnap the princess, will it not?" Flash asked.

The book keeper was stunned; he had not considered this possibility.

"If that is the case then there is no use searching for the princess, if he got her hands on her than she is dead for sure," the book keeper replied sadly.

"Do not lose hope, my friend, we will find her," Flash reassured the old Gnome.

Just then Flash saw a few soldiers rushing into the village. The Captain of the group was carrying someone.

Flash rushed towards the Captain.

"What is it Captain?" Flash asked.

"We have found a dead gnome by the river, General," the Captain replied.

Flash's heart sank, "Who is it? Is it the princess?"

"No, General, he seems to be an ordinary gnome," the Captain replied placing the body on the ground.

"Oh my, it's Gash," the book keeper exclaimed.

"Out of the way, out of the way," said Gnarly, pushing everyone aside.

He stopped dead in his tracks when he saw Gash.

"WHAT IS THE MEANING OF THIS?" Gnarly yelled at the Captain, "who did this to him?"

"We don't know," the Captain replied in an offended tone, "we found him by the river already dead."

"Is that a confession? You left him there after you killed him? Is that what you did with the princess?" Gnarly was shouting at the top of his voice.

"Enough of this," the General raised his voice in response.

"We did not do anything to the princess or this gnome, and you will do well to remember this," Flash warned him.

"Are you threatening me, General? Are you saying that you will kill me too if I don't stop telling the truth?" Gnarly responded to the General's warning.

"That is enough!" the General yelled at Gnarly, "Captain, arrest that gnome," Flash commanded.

The Captain moved forward to carry out the General's orders but Gnarly punched him.

"FIGHTTT!!" yelled Gnarly, "this is the time to avenge the princess and Gash. Fight for your freedom," he continued.

All of a sudden all the gnomes unleashed themselves on the soldiers. It happened so fast that the soldiers had little time to react.

"Protect the GENERAL!!!" the Captain yelled, while fighting off a number of gnomes.

At once a mass of soldiers rushed to defend Flash. Gnarly was, however, closer to the General and he leaped at Flash. Just at that moment Stampy intervened and shoved Gnarly to the ground.

"Signal the reserves," the General ordered in a loud clear voice.

One of the soldiers started waving a red flag signaling the forest guard to move in.

Suddenly horns sounded from all sides and the forest guard started to rush towards the village.

"There are too many of them!" yelled a gnome.

"Keep fighting!" shouted Gnarly with his eyes fixed on Stampy.

The princess, on the other hand, was about to nod off when she heard all the noise.

"What is going on down there?" one gnome asked the other.

"Maybe we should go and check," the other gnome said to his partner and they both set off towards the village.

Gnelissa decided to follow them to the village as there lay the key to her salvation and because she was curious regarding all the noise. All the way to the village she could only think of the various punishments that she would bestow upon Gnarly and his goons. The thought pleased her a great deal. She was also thinking to discuss security with Stampy and Flash when she reached the village. It was clearly a security failure which allowed these gnomes to kidnap her this easily.

She broke away from her thoughts with a start. She was nearing the village and the noise was getting louder and clearer.

"What is happening?" she thought to herself.

"Whoa! They are fighting the villagers," claimed one of the gnomes walking at a considerable distance in front of her.

"The gnomes are outnumbered; we need to go and help them," replied the second gnome and they ran towards to the village.

Gnelissa couldn't believe her ears. Everything was fine as far as she could recall.

"I must put an end to this," she thought to herself while heading towards the village market.

The market seemed to be a mess with gnomes trying to fight off the army but failing miserably. The village soldiers, who were present in large numbers, had surrounded all the gnomes and were ready to discipline them.

The gnomes had taken quite a beating, but were still eyeing the soldiers as if waiting for the right moment to pounce.

The princess realized what was about to happen and rushed forward.

"Stop! Stop! STOPP!" she screamed.

"What is going on here?" she asked angrily.

"Princess," the book keeper exclaimed, "you are alive!"

"Yes, I am, book keeper, but that is not the answer to my question," she replied.

"What is going on here?" Gnelissa asked again.

"Princess, we thought the villagers had killed you so we retaliated," replied a gnome standing next to the book keeper.

"What made you think I was dead?" she asked.

"Well let me guess it was Gnarly, wasn't it?" she asked looking directly at Gnarly.

At that very moment Gnelissa spotted the two gnomes who had kidnapped her.

"Seize those gnomes," she commanded at once.

The gnomes tried to run for it but they were seized by the other members of their tribe.

"Bring them forward," she commanded.

"My people, I was kidnapped by three gnomes. One I killed while trying to run away. I followed these two back to the village," she explained.

"I know perfectly well whose plan it was to get rid of me, and it was not the villagers."

"Who was it then, princess?" asked the book keeper.

"Why don't you ask them?" she said pointing towards the captured gnomes.

One of the gnomes surrounding the prisoners kicked them.

"Who told you to kidnap the princess?" he barked at the prisoners.

"It was Gash who came to us and told us that we have to kidnap the princess as Gnarly wanted to draw a rift between the gnomes and villagers," one of the captured gnomes explained.

"He told us that we were going to kidnap the princess first and then Lola at a later date, so that neither the villagers nor the gnomes would trust each other."

"This will allow Gnarly to become the leader and he intended to take over the village," he continued.

"That's a lie!" Gnarly yelled.

"Silence, Gnarly. I have had enough of your tricks and you have gone too far," the princess replied angrily.

The mood around the village changed suddenly. Everybody was staring at Gnarly, and it seemed they all agreed that Gnarly had crossed the line.

"What does the book say about such an act?" Gnelissa asked turning towards the book keeper, "what should be the punishment for the culprits?"

"The punishment for this crime is equivalent to death or banishment," replied the book keeper.

"Very well then, it is my wish that Gnarly and his accomplices be banished from the tribe for life, however," she turned towards Stampy and Flash, "he was responsible for disturbing the peace of your village, therefore, you have the right to supersede my judgment if you wish."

Flash and Stampy were pleased to see that the princess had returned, however, they were in a bad mood over this entire ordeal. They were angry with the fact that the gnomes had revolted against their authority at the time of the feast.

"We will require a moment to consider this matter, princess," Stampy replied.

"As you wish," the princess said.

"Lola, we will require your say on the matter," Stampy told Lola.

Lola was standing behind several guards who were keeping her out of harm's way. She hopped forward towards Stampy and Flash, and the three of them moved towards a corner in order to discuss the matter.

In the meanwhile the gnomes had captured Gnarly, who seemed very pale at the prospect of eminent death. He did not expect the princess to be lenient with him, but he got lucky with her. Stampy and Flash were an entirely different story. He knew his chances of survival were slim because he had not only insulted the General, but also tried to attack him. As for Stampy he had saved the General and wrestled Gnarly for a brief period. Furthermore, he was sure that

Lola would not be too keen to forgive Gnarly as he had almost gotten her killed, not to mention tried to kidnap her.

He had single handedly offended four influential beings; one of them had decided to banish him, and the other three were deciding his fate. He was sure that he was doomed.

"Lola, we want you to decide the fate of Gnarly," Stampy told Lola.

"Me? You want me to decide?" Lola asked in disbelief.

"Yes, we believe it is only fair that you get to decide the fate of the gnome who plotted to kidnap you and who wanted to take over our village," Stampy replied.

"I know he has done wrong, but we must consider the fact that Gnelissa, whom he tried to kill, has chosen to banish him, not kill him," Lola suggested.

"I believe if we do not consider her judgment then this will make her look weak in front of her people," Lola continued.

"This may, in turn, lead to a revolt among the gnomes in order to overthrow Gnelissa and place a new gnome as the leader, who may not be friendly towards the villagers."

"I think we should strengthen her by allowing her to decide the fate of her people," Lola concluded.

"Very well if that is what you deem correct, then it will be so," Flash replied.

The three off them broke off and moved towards to the crowd. Stampy signaled Lola to move forward and announce their decision.

"We have decided that the fate of the culprits will be decided by the princess," Lola announced.

"We will support her decision; furthermore, all future matters of the gnomes will be handled by the princess, in which she will enjoy our full support."

The princess had not expected this. She understood the importance of this decision, and how it affected her.

Gnarly and the other culprits could not believe their luck; they were going to live a bit longer.

"V-very well then," the princess replied overwhelmed by the decision, "I have decided to banish Gnarly and the other two culprits from the tribe for life."

"They have shamed this tribe and the name of their forefathers, henceforth, they are not members of this tribe and any gnome who comes into contact with them, tries to help them, or befriends them will be considered an enemy of this tribe and will therefore be banished," the princess concluded.

"Captain, escort these culprits out of the village and ensure that they never return to the tribe," commanded Flash.

"Yes, General," responded the Captain, and he along with a small group of soldiers escorted the culprits out of the village.

"Since this is taken care of, I have one more thing to decree," the princess claimed.

"From this moment forth, no gnome is to fight a villager, they should be treated as our family, and their rules are to be respected above all," she told her gnomes.

"I apologize for what happened today," she said turning towards Stampy, Flash and Lola, "I will ensure that it does not happen again."

"We all will ensure that peace prevails and that the two clans live alongside each other peacefully," Stampy added.

"For now, I believe we all must get some rest, for it has been a long night," Stampy continued.

The princess nodded in approval and signaled her people to move towards their encampment.

"Although the gnomes reacted irrationally, they paid the price for it and it seems that this truce will hold for a while," Stampy thought to himself.

"I believe we have finally reached an understanding with the gnomes," Flash said voicing Stampy's thoughts.

"I think so too," Stampy replied as he watched the gnomes walk towards their camp.

Stampy was sure that the princess would hold her end of the bargain now. The gnomes were fully aware that the village army was always prepared for any kind of emergency, and that the villagers had no intention whatsoever to deceive the gnomes.

This understanding was supposed to make all the difference in the world, and Stampy was sure that this peace would survive the test of time.

Bonus Section

Thank you for reading this book. I hope you enjoyed it. Gaming is very near and dear to my heart and I enjoy every moment I spend playing my favourite games.

If you liked this book, and are interested to know more about our other new offerings – guides, tips and tricks, novels etc., I invite you to follow us on Twitter: @innovate_me and connect with us on our website http://www.innovme.com/

If you're a Minecraft fan like I am, I'm sure you'll like my other best-selling releases currently on Amazon.com:

Minecraft Strategy Guides:

1. Awesome Minecraft Building Ideas for You
2. Amazing Minecraft Secrets You Never Knew About
3. The Ultimate Minecraft All-in-one Guide
4. The Ultimate Minecraft Combat Guide For Survival
5. Ten Amazing Fun Mini Games in Minecraft
6. Amazing Minecraft House Designs with step-by-step instruction
7. Awesome Minecraft Traps To Defend Your Home
8. 50 Awesome Minecraft Seeds That You NEED to Know
9. Amazing Minecraft Maps You Will Definitely Enjoy!

Minecraft Novels:

1. The Amazing Tale of Steve: A Minecraft Novel
2. The CRAZY Adventures of Steve: A Minecraft Novel
3. The Amazing Tale of Steve: The Treasures of Block Island
4. Arrival of the Zombies: Minecraft Novel
5. The N00b, The Pig & Herobrine: Minecraft Comic Book
6. The Return of Herobrine: A Minecraft Novel
7. Lost in Minecraft: A Tale of Adventure

Other Novels:

1. The Cursed: A Dark Souls II Fan Fiction Novel
2. Pathfinder: Breaking The Chains of Slavery
3. An Elder Scrolls Epic: Oblivious in Oblivion
4. Watch Dogs: The DedSec Revenge
5. Lego: The Amazing World of Adventure

In my strategy guides, I share neat tips and tricks to help you get better at gaming. From infamous, Clash of Clans, Candy Crush & Dragonvale to Rust & 2048 games, you'll find strategy guides for a wide variety of addictive games.

1. A Beginner's Guide to DOTA 2
2. inFamous Second Son: The Unofficial Strategy Guide
3. Clash of Clans Complete Guide: Gems, Strategies, Tricks and MORE
4. The Last of Us: Amazing Strategies and Secrets
5. Dragonvale: The Complete Guide: Amazing Cheats, Gems, Breeding and MORE!
6. Rust: A Beginner's Guide

If you are interested in reading books on Child development, please take a look at our Toddler's showcase below:

1. Precious Play Time: 50 Ideas To Help You Get The Most Out of The Time You Have With Your Child
2. Happy Toddler: 70 Activities To Calm Your Toddler And Teach Obedience
3. Happy Baby Wise Baby: 70 Activities For Your Child's Development
4. Getting Ready To Sleep: 27 Activities To Calm Your Child
5. A Dad's Book Of Play: 75 Activities To Do With Your Toddler
6. Positive Discipline: 40 activities to encourage positive behavior and beginning social interactions

We also have an awesome Minecraft course on Udemy – an instructor led online learning platform.

1. All about Minecraft: A complete educational course

Have fun gaming!

Egor

Innovate Media

11583830R00047

Printed in Great Britain
by Amazon.co.uk, Ltd.,
Marston Gate.